IMPRESSIONISM

★ IN MY GALLERY ★

WRITTEN BY
EMILIE DUFRESNE

DESIGNED BY
DANIELLE RIPPENGILL

Published in 2022 by Enslow Publishing, LLC
101 W. 23rd Street, Suite 240,
New York, NY 10011

Copyright © 2020 Booklife Publishing
This edition published by arrangement with Booklife Publishing

All rights reserved.

No part of this book may be reproduced by any means without the written permission of the publisher.

Cataloging-in-Publication Data

Names: Dufresne, Emilie.
Title: Impressionism / Emilie Dufresne.
Description: New York : Enslow Publishing, 2022. | Series: In my gallery | Includes glossary and index.
Identifiers: ISBN 9781978524118 (pbk.) | ISBN 9781978524132 (library bound) | ISBN 9781978524125 (6 pack) | ISBN 9781978524149 (ebook)
Subjects: LCSH: Impressionism (Art)--Juvenile literature. | Art, Modern--19th century--Juvenile literature.
Classification: LCC N6465.I4 D843 2022 | DDC 709.03'44--dc23

Designer: Danielle Rippengill
Editor: Madeline Tyler

Printed in the United States of America

CPSIA compliance information: Batch #CS22ENS: For further information contact Enslow Publishing, New York, New York at 1-800-398-2504

IMAGE CREDITS

COVER AND THROUGHOUT – ARTBESOURO, APRIL_PIE, SHTONADO, TASHANATASHA, HAPPYPICTURES, JUDYJUMP, YULIYA DARAFEI. BACKGROUNDS – EXPRESSVECTORS. GABE & ARTISTS – GRINBOX. GALLERY – GOODSTUDIO, SIBERIAN ART. 2 – FOCUS_BELL, GRINBOX, STOCKVECTOR. 5 – SWEET ART. 8 – ONYXPRJ, NOTIONPIC. 9 – KARAKOTSYA, EVERETT – ART. 10&11 – EVERETT – ART. 14&15 – STOCKVECTOR. 17 – NIKITEEV_KONSTANTIN. 18&19 – YULIYA DARAFEI, OLGA_C, SHAKABRA. 22&23 – HASIRU. 28&29 – YULIYA DARAFEI, GRINBOX, OLGABERLET, HASIRU. IMAGES ARE COURTESY OF SHUTTERSTOCK.COM. WITH THANKS TO GETTY IMAGES, THINKSTOCK PHOTO AND ISTOCKPHOTO.

CONTENTS

Page 4   Welcome to the Gallery
Page 5   Types of Art
Page 6   Impressionism Wing
Page 8   What Is Impressionism?
Page 12   Edgar Degas
Page 14   Activity: Still but Moving
Page 16   Claude Monet
Page 18   Activity: Spongy Landscapes
Page 20   Pierre-Auguste Renoir
Page 22   Activity: Watercolors and Wax
Page 24   Mary Cassatt
Page 26   Activity: Pastel Self-Portraits
Page 28   Opening Night
Page 30   Quiz
Page 31   Glossary
Page 32   Index

Words that look like **this** are explained in the glossary on page 31.

WELCOME TO THE GALLERY

Hello, I'm Gabe. I work in this gallery and it is my job to learn about and create artworks in the style of Impressionism.

Museums and Galleries

Museums and galleries are buildings that contain art or **artifacts**. They look after the artworks and show them to the public. They can put on exhibitions and shows to display their art too.

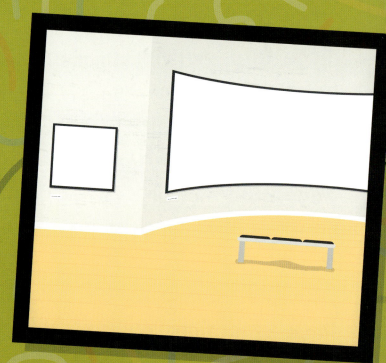

TYPES OF ART

There are lots of different types of art, such as **sculpture**, **installation art**, and **performance art**. The Impressionists were mostly known for their paintings. This means we need to know how to describe the **techniques** that painters use when creating their art.

Brushstrokes are the marks that are made by a tool, such as a paintbrush, being dragged across the **canvas**. There are many different types of brushstrokes, such as short and thick or long and smooth.

Impasto is when paint is layered thickly onto a canvas so that it sticks out from the surface rather than being smooth and flat.

Optical mixing is when an artist puts two colors next to each other on a canvas to give the idea that the colors are mixing rather than mixing them together on a **palette**.

IMPRESSIONISM WING

Welcome to the Impressionism Wing! It may be empty at the moment, but soon this wing will be filled with amazing paintings in the styles of different Impressionist artists.

Some museums or galleries only show one type of art, or art from one particular artist. This gallery has different areas of the building for different art **movements**. This wing will show Impressionist work.

WHAT IS IMPRESSIONISM?

Before Impressionism

Before Impressionism, there was an art movement called Realism. Realist paintings often showed everyday people in everyday positions. Before this, paintings were often of very grand or impressive things and rich people would often pose for the painting.

RICH PERSON POSING

EVERYDAY PERSON DOING EVERYDAY THINGS

Realism was the first movement where working-class people were shown doing everyday things, such as working or cleaning. Realist paintings were often of the city or the countryside, and would show the working class going about their lives.

What Common People Do

Realism influenced Impressionism – Impressionist artists also wanted to show **landscapes** and scenes of everyday things. Impressionism began in Paris in the 1860s. At this time, lots of railway lines were being built to the French countryside from Paris. This meant that artists could travel there to paint.

IMPRESSIONIST LANDSCAPE PAINTING

IMPRESSIONIST PORTRAIT PAINTING

During this time, Paris was changing; more and more **middle-class** people could sit outside and enjoy getting together in the streets. Many Impressionist painters chose to show these scenes in their work. Whether this was eating lunch in a park, having a drink, or walking to work, the everyday was still being shown in Impressionist works.

One Moment in Time

There were some differences between Realism and Impressionism, and one of these was how artists painted these scenes. The Impressionists were not worried about making a scene look real. Instead, they wanted to show what they saw in the blink of an eye or give the impression, or idea, of a moment in time. This is why they became known as the Impressionists.

Impressionist artists also tried to show light in paintings in a different way than how it had been done before. Much like how they wanted to show one moment in time, the Impressionists also wanted to show how they saw light in one moment. This also made the paintings look less like Realist paintings.

Movement and Brushstrokes

Impressionist artists also tried to show movement in their paintings. Rather than being set up or posed, the artists would often paint outside in public spaces. The way they showed light in their paintings helped to give the impression of movement in the painting. Impressionists were also very **revolutionary** in how they put paint onto the canvas. They often used impasto and their short, thick brushstrokes could be seen. The Impressionists were known for using brighter colors than the movements that had come before them.

EDGAR DEGAS

Country of Birth: France
Born: 1834
Died: 1917 (aged 83)

Edgar Degas was born in Paris. He went to a very prestigious school to study art before traveling to Italy to study Renaissance art by artists such as Leonardo da Vinci and Michelangelo.

Degas started as a Realist artist, but he soon began to create paintings of modern life in Paris. He painted scenes at horse races and at the opera. Unlike other Impressionists of the time, Degas would not create landscape paintings. Instead he focused more on people and how they went about their everyday lives. In particular, he liked to show people in unusual positions, such as ballet dancers stretching or women trying on hats. This allowed him to give the impression of lots of movement in his paintings.

Degas was very important in the Impressionist movement and is part of the group of artists who began the Modern Art period. He is believed to have influenced Pablo Picasso and Henri Matisse.

Activity:
STILL BUT MOVING

You will need:

A camera ✓

A printer ✓

Paper ✓

Wax crayons ✓

Let's try to create a piece of art that shows movement and light, just like Degas.

First, you need to take some photos. I am going to take some of me and my friends dancing, but you could take photos of any kind of movement you want, such as people playing sports.

Choose your favorite photo. Now print it in black and white. Use the crayons to color in the picture. Try to use short, thick lines just like the Impressionists did.

Keep looking at the photo to see where the light hits the people's bodies. Use lighter colors such as white and cream where the light falls.

Don't worry about coloring inside the lines. Impressionist paintings often looked blurry because they were trying to show movement.

Next, I'll add more light colors to really make it look like a fleeting moment, and then I'm finished!

CLAUDE MONET

Country of Birth: France
Born: 1840
Died: 1926 (aged 86)

Claude Monet is seen as the pioneer and leader of Impressionism. Although Monet began painting people, he is mostly known for his landscape paintings. He often painted "en plein air" which means "in open air" in French. He would often choose one subject, such as haystacks, cathedrals, or waterlilies, and then paint them over and over again. He would paint them at different times of day and in different types of weather. This changed how the natural light made the landscape look. Throughout his career, Monet painted around 250 paintings just of waterlilies.

Many people see Monet as a very important figure in Modern Art, who changed the way artists expressed themselves in paintings forever by becoming more abstract and expressive in the way he painted.

Activity:
SPONGY LANDSCAPES

You will need:

- Thick paper in any size you want ☑
- Something hard and flat to lean on ☑
- Sponges ☑
- Paints in different colors ☑
- Paintbrushes ☑

It's time to grab your paint and equipment. We are off to paint en plein air!

First, put all the things you need into a bag and go outside – this could be the local park, a forest, or your garden.

I have used this very big piece of paper because I want this to be a large painting that stretches across the curved wall of the gallery, but you can use any size you want. Now use your sponges to paint the background. I'm painting a picture of some boats on a lake, so I am mostly mixing blues and greens on my background.

Once your background is dry, get your paintbrushes out and add in some more detail. There were some boats on the lake and some buildings to the right, so I will add those in with paint. What details could you add to your painting?

PIERRE-AUGUSTE RENOIR

Country of Birth: France
Born: 1841
Died: 1919 (aged 78)

Pierre-Auguste Renoir began painting pottery in a factory before moving to Paris to study painting techniques. While studying, he met Claude Monet. It was not long until Renoir's work began to change and look more Impressionist. Like Degas, Renoir's Impressionist paintings were often of people outside and living their modern lives. In his work, he tried to show that sunlight falling on people's skin looked luminous or glowing, and sunlight falling though the leaves of plants looked as though it was sparkling.

Later in his career, Renoir stopped creating Impressionist artworks and his work changed. Instead of using short brushstrokes, he began to create paintings with stronger and clearer edges to all the objects. However, he still used light colors, which he got from the Impressionists.

Activity:
WATERCOLORS AND WAX

You will need:

- Wax crayons ✓
- A glass of water ✓
- Watercolor paints ✓
- Paintbrushes ✓
- Thick paper or cardboard ✓
- A camera ✓

We are going to try to create a painting in the style of Renoir using a technique called **wax resist**.

Go outside to a space with some nice plants or trees. Take a photo of your friends or people you know near the plants. When you're back inside, get ready to draw.

First, **sketch** out a drawing of the picture. Use the wax crayons to color in the picture, but not the background. Make sure you add in any details you want to stand out using the crayons.

Once you are happy with your drawing, get your watercolors. Choose the colors you want to be in your background. Brush them across your whole painting. Don't be nervous about painting over the wax crayons – the crayons will resist the paint! Once you are happy, let your painting dry. Now you have a painting in the style of Renoir!

MARY CASSATT

Country of Birth: U.S.
Born: 1844
Died: 1926 (aged 82)

Mary Cassatt was born in the U.S. but travelled to Europe to study. She created art while travelling and had one of her pieces accepted at an exhibition. Edgar Degas saw the exhibition and asked her to show her work alongside the Impressionists.

Cassatt preferred to show people instead of landscapes in her artwork. However, her pieces of people were different from other Impressionist works of the time. Cassatt chose to show women from inside their homes in her artworks. She showed mothers and children sitting together, or women reading or having tea.

Cassatt helped to spread the ideas of Impressionism from Europe to the U.S. She would ask her friends in the U.S. to buy Impressionist artworks from Europe. In fact, many of these works make up part of a collection in the Metropolitan Museum in New York City.

Activity:
PASTEL SELF-PORTRAITS

You will need:

- Pastels in various colors ☑
- A pencil ☑
- Thick paper or cardboard ☑
- A camera ☑
- A friend ☑

Mary Cassatt was known for using pastels to create her pieces. Let's try to create a self-portrait using Cassatt's techniques!

Sit down and do something that you do a lot, such as having a snack or looking at your tablet or computer. Try not to pose – just sit as you usually would. Get a friend to take a picture of you doing this.

Now recreate your photo. First, sketch it out using your pencil. Once you are happy with your sketch, it's time to get your pastels out. Cassatt was known for using light colors, so I'm going to use light colors too. The fun thing about pastels is you can use your fingers to mix colors together or layer them.

I have blurred some white bits into the other colors using my finger, just like the Impressionists did. Now I just need to finish off adding in the other colors and it will be ready for the gallery!

OPENING NIGHT

How do you think the wing looks now that it's full of art? It's great to see everyone talking about the artworks! Let's see what they are saying...

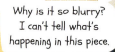

There are no right or wrong answers when you are talking about a piece of art, or how it makes you feel. What do you think of these pieces? Which is your favorite, and why? Are there any that make you feel happy or sad?

I love the difference between the watercolor and the wax.

Yes! The wax really stands out and makes the painting almost sparkle.

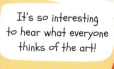
It's so interesting to hear what everyone thinks of the art!

Why do you think they used pastels in this one and not paint?

I don't think they could blend the colors in that interesting way with just paint.

29

QUIZ

1. What art movement came before Impressionism?
2. Around what time did galleries stop showing all their paintings at once?
3. Which artist liked to show people moving in unusual positions?
4. Who was known for painting landscapes en plein air?
5. Which artist was known for using pastels to create their works?

Answers: 1. Realism 2. Mid-1800s 3. Edgar Degas 4. Claude Monet 5. Mary Cassatt

You could try to go to a gallery or museum near you.

It might **inspire** you to create some more art. There are loads of different art movements and styles to try. You could even find your own way of creating art and start a whole new movement! Don't forget to ask the people you are with how the artworks make them feel.

GLOSSARY

abstract — describing art that doesn't try to show something as it looks in real life

artifacts — objects made by humans in history

canvas — a woven fabric that is pulled tightly over a frame to create a blank space to be painted on

expressive — showing feelings and emotions

inspire — to influence to do something

installation art — art that people have to interact with by either walking around, touching, or listening to

landscapes — scenes that include nature, such as fields, mountains, or oceans

middle-class — describing people who are in between the upper class and working class

Modern Art — an art movement from around 1850 to 1970 that includes many art styles and represents when artists began moving away from traditional art

movements — categories or types of art that an artwork or artist might belong to, which can sometimes be related to a certain time or place

palette — a piece of equipment that an artist may use to mix colors

performance art — a type of art that is often performed live for viewers or spectators

pioneer — the first person to do something new or in a new way

portrait — a painting, drawing, or photograph of a person

pose — to hold yourself in a certain way for a period of time, usually for a photograph or painting

prestigious — having an important and highly regarded status

Renaissance — a period of time from the 14th to the 17th century when European art and literature became popular again

revolutionary — doing something in a way that completely changes how it was done or thought of before

sculpture — a decorative object made through carving, chiseling, or molding

sketch — to do a quick drawing, often in pencil

techniques — particular ways of doing something

wax resist — an art technique that involves using wax crayons to draw a picture before painting over it with watercolors; the wax resists the watercolor paint and the picture can be seen through the paint

working-class — describing people who make up the main workforce in a society

INDEX

B
brushstrokes 5, 11, 20

C
canvases 5, 11

D
da Vinci, Leonardo 12

F
France 9, 12, 16, 20

G
galleries 4, 6–7, 19, 27, 30

I
impasto 5, 11
Italy 12

L
landscapes 9, 12, 16, 24

M
Matisse, Henri 12
Michelangelo 12

Modern Art 12, 16
museums 4, 6, 24, 30

O
optical mixing 5

P
pastels 26–27, 29
Picasso, Pablo 12
portraits 9, 26

R
Realism 8–10, 12
Renaissance 12

S
sketching 23, 27

U
U.S. 24

W
watercolors 22–23, 29